This edition first published in 1993 by
Sunburst Books, Deacon House, 65 Old Church Street,
London, SW3 5BS

Copyright © Editorial LIBSA, Narciso Serra, 25 – Tel 433 54 07 –
28007 MADRID
4.ª EDICION 1991
Copyright English language text © 1993 Sunburst Books

ISBN 1 85778 003 5

Printed and bound in China

VEGETARIAN COOKING

CONTENTS

INTRODUCTION

The idea of a diet based exclusively on vegetable products is not new - in fact it can be traced back to ancient civilisations. However, it has continued to develop over the years, and today's vegetarian diet offers a far broader range of options and a much healthier approach for those who prefer not to eat any form of meat.

In reality, most vegetarians admit a few complementary, animal-based products into their diet, such as eggs and milk and other dairy products. In this instance a vegetarian diet doesn't present any nutritional problems, since it contains a sufficient amount of the essential amino acids, minerals and vitamins to sustain the vital body functions of subsistence, growth and reproduction.

But it can be difficult to address the problems faced by pure vegetarians who don't eat any other products, as a diet which consists solely of vegetable proteins may often be lacking in those essential minerals and vitamins, particularly calcium and B12, which can lead to deficiency syndromes. Furthermore, vegetables contain large amounts of water and cellulose, which can over-stimulate the digestive system, causing a loss of nutrients.

The key to a healthy vegetarian lifestyle, as demonstrated in this book, lies in a balanced diet. Meals should include a substantial quantity of those foodstuffs which contain the most concentrated fat and proteins - such as nuts and dried fruits - and, above all, a variety of different types of vegetable protein.

Vegetarian Cooking contains an imaginative collection of delicious vegetarian recipes, designed to provide the non-meat eater with a balanced, healthy diet, with the maximum taste, texture and variety.

Note: Some of the recipes in this book include eggs, milk and other dairy products.

SALADS

CABBAGE SALAD

Serves 4

200 g/1½ lb white cabbage
200 g/1½ lb red cabbage
3 carrots
2 celery sticks
4 tbsp virgin olive oil
1 tbsp lemon juice
2 tbsp chopped parsley

Wash and finely chop the white and red cabbage. Peel and grate the carrots and chop the celery. Mix all the vegetables and season with the oil and lemon juice. Sprinkle with the chopped parsley and serve.

SICILIAN SALAD

Serves 4

3 medium-sized tomatoes
1 cucumber
1 onion
3 tbsp virgin olive oil
1 tbsp chopped oregano
salt

Wash and slice the tomatoes and cucumber. Peel and slice the onion. Place the vegetables in a salad bowl and season with the oil, oregano and salt. Leave to stand for at least 1 hour before serving.

LEEK SALAD

Serves 4

12 leeks
3 tbsp virgin olive oil
squeeze of lemon juice
2 tbsp chopped parsley

Remove and discard the roots and outer leaves of the leeks. Cook the leeks in boiling salted water until barely tender, drain and leave to cool. Arrange the leeks in a serving dish and dress with the oil and lemon juice. Sprinkle over the chopped parsley and serve.

GREEN SALAD

Serves 4

2 cucumbers
1 lettuce
2 green peppers
bunch of watercress
½ celery head
150 ml/5 fl oz yoghurt
squeeze of lemon juice
salt

Wash all the vegetables. Slice the cucumbers thinly and chop the remaining vegetables finely. Place the vegetables in a salad bowl and dress with a sauce made with the yoghurt, lemon juice and a pinch of salt.

EMMENTAL CHEESE SALAD

Serves 4

1 lettuce
2 carrots
100 g/4 oz Emmental cheese
2 tbsp single cream
juice of ½ lemon
ground pepper
salt
1 hard boiled egg
1 tbsp chopped parsley

Wash the lettuce and cut into shreds. Peel the carrots and cut into strips. Cut the cheese into strips and combine with the vegetables. Dress the salad with a sauce made with the cream, lemon juice, pepper and salt. Chop the hard-boiled egg and sprinkle over with the parsley before serving.

CHEESE AND MUSHROOM SALAD

Serves 4

200 g/7 oz Parmesan cheese
½ lettuce
1 small onion, peeled
1 small celery head
150 g/5 oz mushrooms
50 g/2 oz capers
75 ml/3 fl oz virgin olive oil
2 tbsp lemon juice

Slice the cheese, mushrooms and onion, chop the celery and cut the lettuce into strips then place in a salad bowl with the capers. Mix well and toss with the oil and lemon juice and a little salt.

BEETROOT SALAD WITH MUSTARD SAUCE

Serves 4

½ kg/1 lb cooked beetroot
3 radishes
4 "Petit Suisse" cheeses
1 tbsp mustard
squeeze of lemon juice
pepper & salt

Peel and grate the beetroot. Cut the radishes into quarters. In a salad bowl, mix together the "Petit Suisse", mustard, lemon juice and salt and pepper. Add the beetroot and radishes and serve.

RAW GRATED BEETROOT SALAD

Serves 4

2 medium-sized raw beetroots
1 apple
2 tbsp single cream
squeeze of lemon juice
salt
ground pepper

Peel and grate the beetroot, either by hand or in a food processor. Peel and grate the apple. Mix together and dress with the cream, lemon juice, salt and pepper.

Top: Leek Salad
Bottom: Beetroot Salad with Mushroom Sauce

SALAD NICOISE

Serves 4

1 lettuce
¼ kg/½ lb green beans
6 small potatoes
6 small tomatoes
75 ml/3 fl oz virgin olive oil
2 tbsp sherry vinegar
salt
1 x 12 oz can of tuna
50 g/2 oz black olives
2 tbsp capers

Wash and dry the lettuce leaves and arrange in a salad bowl. Cook the beans in boiling salted water until just tender. Drain and chop. Cook the potatoes, drain and cut into cubes. Cut the tomatoes into quarters and add to the bowl with the beans and potatoes. Dress the vegetables with oil, vinegar and salt and toss well together. Flake the tuna on top of the vegetables and garnish with the olives and capers.

CUCUMBER AND MINT SALAD

Serves 4

3 cucumbers
large sprig fresh mint
100 ml/4 fl oz single cream
salt and pepper

Wash the cucumbers, slice them finely, place in a colander and sprinkle with salt. Leave for 30 minutes to draw out the moisture. Chop the fresh mint. Make a dressing in a salad bowl with the cream, salt, pepper and chopped mint. Rinse and drain the cucumbers and add to the dressing in the bowl.

SANTANDER SALAD

Serves 4

1 small red cabbage
2 apples
3 tbsp virgin olive oil
1 tbsp cider vinegar
pinch of dried tarragon
salt

Wash the red cabbage, then chop very finely and place in a salad bowl. Quarter the apples, remove the core, slice and add to the cabbage. Dress with a sauce made with the oil, vinegar, tarragon and salt.

Opposite: Cucumber and Mint Salad
Above: Santander Salad

AMERICAN SALAD

Serves 4

3 sweetcorn cobs
1/2 white cabbage
225 ml/8 fl oz mayonnaise
salt

Cook the sweetcorn in boiling salted water until tender. Drain and leave to cool. Shred the cabbage. When the sweetcorn has cooled, remove the corn from the cob and place in a salad bowl with the cabbage. Add the mayonnaise and salt, mix well together and chill until ready to serve.

CELERY AND WALNUT SALAD

Serves 4

2 celery heads
100 g/4 oz shelled walnuts
virgin olive oil
lemon juice
salt & ground pepper
4 tbsp mayonnaise

Cut the celery sticks into thin strips and place in a salad bowl. Finely chop the walnuts, add to the celery and season with oil, lemon juice, salt and pepper. Leave to stand for 1 hour. Just before serving, add the mayonnaise and garnish with shredded lettuce and walnut halves, if desired.

ARTICHOKE SALAD

Serves 4

1 lettuce
4 small cooked artichokes
50 g/2 oz black olives
3 tbsp virgin olive oil
1 tbsp sherry vinegar
1/2 garlic clove, peeled and crushed

Wash the lettuce, cut into shreds and place in a salad bowl. Quarter the artichokes and add to the bowl with the olives. Dress the salad with a sauce made with the oil, vinegar, garlic and a little salt.

ALEXIS SALAD

Serves 4

3 medium-sized carrots
1 chicory
1 celery stalk, finely sliced
1 tbsp finely chopped parsley

salt and white pepper
4 tbsp virgin olive oil
1 tbsp sherry vinegar

Peel and shred the carrots and place in the centre of a serving dish. Wash and dry the chicory leaves and arrange around the carrot. Garnish with the celery and parsley. Season with salt and pepper and dress the salad with the oil and vinegar.

Opposite, top: American Salad
Opposite, bottom: Celery and Walnut Salad
Above, top: Artichoke Salad
Above, bottom: Alexis Salad

MUSHROOM SALAD

Serves 4

1/2 kg/1 lb mushrooms
salt and ground white pepper
3 tbsp virgin olive oil
1 tbsp sherry vinegar
150 ml/5 fl oz yoghurt

Wipe the mushrooms clean, slice thinly and place in a salad bowl. Season with the salt, pepper, oil and vinegar. Stir well and chill for 1-2 hours. Just before serving, beat the yoghurt and pour over the salad.

COUNTRY SALAD

Serves 4

1/4 kg/1/2 lb runner beans
1 small cauliflower
3 tbsp virgin olive oil
1 tbsp sherry vinegar
salt

Divide the cauliflower into florets and slice the beans. Cook them separately in boiling water until just tender. Drain and place the cauliflower in a salad bowl and arrange the green beans around the outside. Dress the salad with a vinaigrette made with the oil, vinegar and a little salt.

FENNEL SALAD

Serves 4

2 fennel bulbs
2 tomatoes
150 g/5 oz cooked long-grain rice
50 g/2 oz stoned black olives
1 tbsp capers
225 ml/8 fl oz mayonnaise
salt and pepper

Wash the fennel and cut into thin strips. Slice the tomatoes then arrange in a salad bowl with the fennel, rice, olives and capers. Chill before serving. Season the mayonnaise with salt and pepper and serve separately.

GARDEN SALAD

Serves 4

2 bunches watercress
1 small head celery
2 tomatoes
3 tbsp virgin olive oil
salt

Wash the watercress and cut the stalks off. Chop the celery, slice the tomatoes and arrange on a serving dish with the watercress. Dress with the oil and salt.

Below, top: Mushroom Salad
Below, bottom: Country Salad
Opposite, top: Fennel Salad
Opposite, bottom: Garden Salad

SWEETCORN AND BEAN SPROUT SALAD

Serves 4

3 sweetcorn cobs
4 tbsp virgin olive oil
1¹/₂ tbsp lemon juice
salt and pepper
sprig of mint, chopped
1 spring onion, sliced
100 g/4 oz bean sprouts

Cook the sweetcorn cobs in boiling salted water until tender. Drain and allow to cool. Make a vinaigrette in a salad bowl with the oil, lemon juice, salt and pepper. Remove the sweetcorn kernels from the cob and add to the vinaigrette. Stir in the chopped mint, sliced spring onion and bean sprouts. Mix well and leave to stand for 3 hours before serving.

ENDIVE SALAD

Serves 4

1 curly endive
2 tomatoes
3 cooked artichoke hearts
1 small green pepper
2 hard-boiled eggs
3 tbsp olive oil
1 tbsp lemon juice
salt

Clean and chop the endive and place in a salad bowl. Slice the tomatoes, artichoke hearts and green pepper. Halve the eggs, chop the whites and reserve the yolks. Arrange the sliced tomatoes, artichokes and pepper on top of the endive and dress with a sauce made with the oil, lemon juice, salt and yolks of the hard-boiled eggs.

COURGETTE SALAD

Serves 4

¹/₂ kg/1 lb courgettes
4 tbsp virgin olive oil
1 tbsp chopped mint
1 tbsp lemon juice
salt

Cook the courgettes until just tender, drain and slice thickly. Place in a salad bowl and season with the oil, lemon juice and salt. Mix well. Sprinkle with the chopped mint and serve.

Left: Sweetcorn and Beansprout Salad
Right: Endive Salad

MULTICOLOURED SALAD

Serves 4

½ white cabbage
½ red cabbage
2 tomatoes
2 cucumbers
1 celery head
50 g/2 oz mushrooms
⅓ litre/½ pint yoghurt
1 tbsp chopped parsley and oregano
pinch of nutmeg

Clean and chop the cabbage. Slice the tomatoes, cucumbers, celery and mushrooms. Place all the vegetables in a salad bowl and season with the yoghurt mixed with the parsley, oregano and nutmeg.

CHICORY SALAD

Serves 4

3 heads of chicory
100 g/4 oz hard cheese (e.g.Cheddar)
3 tbsp mayonnaise
1 tbsp chopped parsley

Clean the chicory, separate into leaves and arrange on a serving dish. Spoon over the mayonnaise. Cube the cheese, add to the salad and sprinkle with the chopped parsley. Garnish with halved baby tomatoes, if desired.

AUTUMN SALAD

Serves 6

½ kg/1 lb potatoes
¼ kg/½ lb mushrooms
2 bananas
3 Cox's Pippin apples
100 g/4 oz chopped walnuts
50 g/2 oz butter
mayonnaise

Cook the potatoes whole and leave to cool. Chop the mushrooms and sauté in the butter until just cooked. Peel and thinly slice the bananas and apples. Peel and slice the cooled potatoes and place in a salad bowl. Add the mushrooms and chopped fruit. Pour over the mayonnaise, sprinkle with the chopped walnuts and serve.

SUMMER SALAD

Serves 4

¼ kg/½ lb carrots
¼ kg/½ lb turnips
bunch of small radishes
½ lettuce
200 ml/7 fl oz single cream
1 tbsp mustard
squeeze of lemon juice
salt and ground white pepper
2 egg yolks
2 tbsp chopped chives

Peel the carrots and turnips and cut into strips. Wash the radishes and slice thinly. Wash the lettuce and shred finely. Heat the cream in a saucepan and allow to cook for 5 minutes. Add the mustard and lemon juice and season with salt and pepper. Beat the egg yolks and add to the sauce, but do not allow to boil. Place the vegetables in a salad bowl, sprinkle with the chopped chives and serve with the hot sauce.

SOUPS

WATERCRESS SOUP

Serves 4

50 g/2 oz butter
2 onions, peeled and chopped
2 potatoes, peeled and chopped
2 bunches watercress, stalks removed
³/4 litre/1¹/2 pints vegetable stock
salt and pepper

Heat the butter in a saucepan and sauté the onions and potatoes. Chop half the watercress and set aside. Add the remaining watercress to the pan and cook over a low heat for a few more minutes. Add the stock and season with salt and pepper. Cover and cook over a low heat for about 20 minutes, until the vegetables are tender. Remove from the heat, leave to cool and blend in a liquidiser or food processor. Pour into a bowl and chill well. Just before serving stir in the reserved chopped watercress.

CELERY SOUP

Serves 4

2 tbsp olive oil
2 celery heads, chopped
2 litres/3¹/2 pints vegetable stock
75 g/3 oz brown rice
salt and pepper
100 g/4 oz hard cheese (e.g. Cheddar), grated

Heat the oil in a saucepan and sauté the celery over a low heat for 5 minutes. Add the stock and the rice, cover and simmer for about 45 minutes until the rice is cooked. Season to taste and serve with the grated cheese.

LEEK AND TAPIOCA SOUP

Serves 4

2 tbsp oil
1 onion, peeled and sliced
1 tbsp flour
1 litre/2 pints boiling water
3 leeks, peeled and sliced
3 tbsp tapioca
salt and pepper
2 tbsp chopped parsley

Heat the oil in a saucepan and sauté the onion over a low heat for 2 minutes. Add the flour, stir well and add the water. Bring to the boil over a medium heat and then simmer for 20 minutes until the leeks are tender. Add the tapioca. Cook over a high heat for a few minutes. Season to taste, sprinkle with the chopped parsley and serve.

Opposite, top: Multicoloured Salad
Opposite, bottom: Chicory Salad
Left, top: Watercress Soup
Left, bottom: Celery Soup

ALMOND GAZPACHO

Serves 4

50 g/2 oz almonds
1 garlic clove, peeled
salt
75 g/3 oz crustless white bread
4 tbsp virgin olive oil
1 tbsp sherry vinegar
1 litre/1 ¾ pints cold water

Place the almonds, garlic and a little salt in a mortar and pound with a pestle until a paste is obtained. Dip the bread in cold water, drain, then add to the mixture and blend all the ingredients. Gradually add the oil, stirring constantly, until the mixture is the consistency of mayonnaise. Add the vinegar. Pour the mixture into a large bowl and gradually add the cold water, stirring. Serve cold. This soup can also be made in a blender or food processor.

AVOCADO SOUP

Serves 4

3 avocados
squeeze of lemon juice
300ml/¹/₂ pint yoghurt
³/₄ litre/1¹/₂ pints vegetable stock
salt and pepper

Cut the avocados in half, remove the stones and spoon out the flesh into a mixing bowl. Mash the avocado flesh and sprinkle with lemon juice. Then add the yoghurt and stock and season with salt and pepper. Pour the mixture into a blender or food processor and blend to a purée. Chill before serving.

RICE SOUP

Serves 4

80 g/3½ oz rice
1 litre/1 ¾ pints vegetable stock
olive oil
2 tomatoes, peeled and chopped
1 garlic clove, peeled and chopped

1 dessertspoon chopped mint

Simmer the rice in the vegetable stock for 15 minutes. Meanwhile, heat the oil in a frying pan and sauté the tomatoes, garlic and mint for 5 minutes. Add to the rice and stock mixture and simmer for 5 minutes until the rice is cooked. Season and serve hot.

Opposite: Almond Gazpacho
Below: Avocado Soup

GARLIC SOUP

Serves 4

4 tbsp oil
4 garlic cloves, peeled and finely chopped
250 g/8 oz bread, cubed
1 teaspoon cayenne pepper
1½ litres/2½ pints boiling water
salt

Heat the oil in a saucepan and fry the garlic until golden. Add the bread and cayenne and cook for 2 minutes, stirring constantly. Add the boiling water, season with salt then simmer over a low heat for 15 minutes. Serve immediately.

PEPPER AND TOMATO SOUP

Serves 4

4 tbsp olive oil
1 onion, peeled and chopped
½ kg/1 lb peppers, deseeded and chopped
½ kg/1 lb tomatoes, peeled and chopped
1½ litres/2½ pints boiling water

Heat the oil in a saucepan and sauté the onion until it is just turning golden. Add the chopped peppers and cook over a low heat until almost tender. Add the chopped tomatoes and continue cooking until the peppers are soft. Purée the mixture in a blender or food processor then tip back into the pan and add the boiling water. Season with salt and pepper and cook over a low heat for 10 minutes.

GAZPACHO

Serves 4

150 g/5 oz crustless bread
1 kg/2.2 lb tomatoes, peeled and chopped
1 cucumber, peeled and chopped
1 pepper, deseeded and chopped
5 tbsp olive oil
2 tbsp sherry vinegar
salt
1 litre/1¾ pints water

Soak the bread in a little water, then squeeze out the excess liquid and place the bread in a blender or food processor. Add the remaining ingredients, except the water, and blend to a purée. Add the water and blend again. Serve chilled.

ONION SOUP

Serves 4

4 tbsp oil
½ kg/1 lb onions, peeled and sliced
2 tbsp flour
2 litres/3½ pints vegetable stock
salt and pepper
250 g/8 oz sliced bread
100 g/4 oz Cheddar cheese, grated

Heat the oil in a saucepan and sauté the onions until just turning golden. Add the flour, stir well, then pour in the stock and cook over a low heat for 10 minutes. Taste and adjust the seasoning.

Meanwhile, toast the bread slices. Pour the soup into an ovenproof dish, top with the pieces of toasted bread and the grated cheese. Bake in the oven at 220°C/425°F/gas mark 7 for 5 minutes.

SPINACH AND OATMEAL SOUP

Serves 4

olive oil
2 onions, peeled and sliced
1 kg/2.2 lb spinach, cooked and drained
6 tbsp oatmeal
1 litre/1¾ pints water
¼ litre/7 fl oz milk
1 tsp soya sauce
salt

Heat the oil in a saucepan and sauté the onions until just softened. Add the cooked spinach, oatmeal and water then cover and cook for 20 minutes. Stir in the milk then blend the mixture to a purée in a blender or food processor. Reheat the soup, season with the soya sauce and salt and serve immediately.

LEEK SOUP

Serves 4

¼ kg/½ lb leeks, chopped
½ kg/1 lb potatoes, peeled and chopped
½ litre/¾ pint hot milk
25 g/1 oz butter
salt and pepper

Place the chopped leeks and potatoes in a large saucepan with just enough cold water to cover. Simmer, covered, for about 30 minutes. Purée the mixture in a blender or food processor then pour it back into the pan. Add the hot milk and continue to cook for a further 5 minutes,

stirring constantly. Season, stir in the butter and serve.

MINESTRONE SOUP

Serves 4

75 g/3 oz peas
¼ kg/½ lb potatoes, peeled and cubed
¼ kg/½ lb watercress, chopped
1 leek, sliced
1 aubergine, cubed
1 celery stick, sliced
2 tomatoes, peeled and chopped
1 litre/2 pints water
1 tbsp chopped basil
1 tbsp chopped parsley
1 tbsp olive oil
150 g/5 oz pasta shells
salt and pepper
50 g/2 oz grated Parmesan cheese

Place all the vegetables in a saucepan with the water. Bring to the boil, cover and simmer for 20 minutes until just tender.

Meanwhile, pound together the herbs and olive oil to make a paste. Add the pasta shells and herb paste to the vegetables and continue cooking for 10 minutes. Season well and serve sprinkled with the Parmesan cheese.

ENDIVE SOUP

Serves 4

75 g/3 oz butter
½ kg/1 lb chicory, chopped
1½ litres/2½ pints vegetable stock
½ kg/1 lb potatoes, peeled and cubed
salt and pepper
¼ litre/8 fl oz hot milk

Heat half the butter in a saucepan and sauté the chopped chicory until it begins to turn golden. Add the stock and potatoes and season with salt and pepper. Cover and simmer for 20 minutes until the potatoes are cooked. Stir in the hot milk and cook for a few more seconds. Add the remaining butter and serve garnished with chopped parsley, if desired.

Top: Minestrone Soup
Bottom: Endive Soup

VEGETABLES

CURRIED COURGETTES

Serves 4

4 medium-sized courgettes, trimmed and quartered
100 g/4 oz butter
1 onion, peeled and finely chopped
2 tbsp flour
2-3 tsp curry powder
300ml/½ pint milk
salt and pepper

Place the courgettes in a large saucepan with half the butter. Add just enough water to cover them and cook, covered, until the water has evaporated. Meanwhile, sauté the onion in the remaining butter. Add the flour and curry powder and mix well. Stir in the milk, season with salt and pepper and cook for a few minutes. Blend the mixture to a purée in a blender or food processor.

When the courgettes are cooked and all the water has evaporated, pour in the curry sauce, heat for a few minutes and serve.

CHOPPED PEPPERS AND AUBERGINES

Serves 4

3 large red peppers
2 aubergines
1 garlic clove, peeled and crushed
5 tbsp lemon juice
salt

Remove the stalks from the peppers and aubergines. Place under a grill and cook, turning frequently, until the skins are blistered and black. Allow to cool slightly, then peel the vegetables and remove the seeds from the peppers. Chop the vegetables, place in a salad bowl and dress with a vinaigrette made with the crushed garlic, lemon juice and oil. Leave to stand for 30 minutes before serving.

Left: Curried Courgettes
Right: Chopped Peppers and Aubergines

GREEN BEANS IN CREAM

Serves 4

1 kg/2.2 lb green beans
1 garlic clove, peeled and crushed
50 g/2 oz butter
200 ml/7 fl oz single cream
1 tbsp parsley
salt and pepper

Cook the green beans in boiling, salted water until just tender. Drain and set aside. Sauté the garlic in the butter, add the cream and cook over a low heat for a few minutes, stirring constantly. Season with salt and pepper, add the cooked green beans and heat together for a few minutes, stirring occasionally. Sprinkle with the chopped parsley and serve immediately.

VEGETABLE PUDDING

Serves 4

200 g/7 oz celery, finely chopped
2 carrots, peeled and grated
300 g/10 oz cottage cheese, sieved
50 g/2 oz stoned black olives, chopped
pinch of grated nutmeg
salt and pepper
extra olives, to garnish

Place all the ingredients in a mixing bowl and stir well to combine. Turn the mixture into 4 individual ramekin dishes or 1 medium-sized dish, then chill in the refrigerator for 1 hour. Turn out and decorate with olives.

GREEK-STYLE FENNEL

Serves 4

2 bulbs of fennel
olive oil
2 onions, peeled and chopped
6 tomatoes, peeled and chopped
1 fresh bouquet garni (thyme, bay leaf and parsley)
1 garlic clove, peeled and crushed
100 ml/4 fl oz dry white wine
juice of 2 lemons
salt and pepper

Heat the oil in a large saucepan and sauté the chopped onion until soft. Add the tomatoes, bouquet garni, garlic, white wine and lemon juice. Season with salt and pepper and cook over a low heat for 15 minutes. Meanwhile blanch the fennel strips in boiling water for a few minutes. Drain, refresh under cold running water then add to the sauce. Cover and cook for a further 30 minutes. Allow to cool, then chill and serve very cold.

Top: Green Beans in Cream
Bottom: Vegetable Pudding

STUFFED ARTICHOKES

Serves 4

6 small artichokes
squeeze of lemon juice
3 tbsp oil
4 tomatoes, peeled and chopped
1 aubergine, cubed
1 celery stalk, sliced
salt
100 g/4 oz stoned black olives, chopped
3 tbsp breadcrumbs

Clean the artichokes, remove the stalks, the outer leaves and the tips. Bring a large saucepan of salted water to the boil, add the artichokes and a squeeze of lemon juice and simmer for about 30 minutes until the artichokes are tender. Drain and set aside. Heat the oil in a frying pan, add the tomatoes, aubergine and celery, season with salt, and sauté until the vegetables are cooked. Add the chopped olives and mix in well. Arrange the artichokes in an ovenproof dish greased with oil and fill them with the fried vegetable mixture. Sprinkle over the breadcrumbs and brown in the oven at 220°C/425°F/gas mark 7 for a few minutes.

VEGETABLE CHOP SUEY

Serves 4

3 carrots, peeled
2 cucumbers
3 tbsp olive oil
2 onions, peeled and sliced
3 peppers, deseeded and sliced
3 courgettes, cubed
2 tomatoes, peeled and chopped
1 tsp coriander
1 tsp cinnamon
1 tsp ginger

Cut the carrots and cucumbers into thick matchsticks. Heat the oil in a frying pan and sauté the onions, peppers, carrots and cucumbers for 10 minutes. Add the courgettes, tomatoes and mushrooms, season with the spices, cook for 2 minutes then stir in the soya sauce and serve.

POTATO AND CHEESE SOUFFLÉ

Serves 4

6 medium-sized potatoes, peeled
350 ml/12 fl oz hot milk
4 eggs, separated
1 tsp flour

25 g/4 oz grated Parmesan cheese
salt and pepper

Cook the potatoes in boiling, salted water, drain and mash well, gradually adding the hot milk. Beat the egg yolks in a mixing bowl, add the flour, grated cheese and salt and pepper then stir into the puréed potatoes. Beat the egg whites until stiff and fold into the potato mixture. Pour into a greased soufflé dish and bake in the oven at 180°C/350°F/gas mark 4 for 20 minutes.

COURGETTES STUFFED WITH SPINACH

Serves 4

6 courgettes
75 g/3 oz butter
1 onion, peeled and finely chopped
salt and pepper
1 kg/2.2 lb spinach, cooked, drained and chopped
2 garlic cloves, peeled and crushed
1 tbsp chopped parsley
50 g/2 oz grated Parmesan cheese
75 g/3 oz breadcrumbs

Cut the courgettes in half lengthways and scoop out the flesh. Chop the flesh and set aside.
Heat half the butter in a small frying pan and sauté the onion for 2 minutes, then add the courgette flesh and salt and pepper. Cook over a high heat until all the moisture has evaporated.
Heat the remaining butter in a frying pan and sauté the spinach, garlic and parsley for 2 minutes, stirring. Mix the spinach with the courgette flesh, add the cheese and stir well. Fill the hollowed-out courgettes with this mixture and sprinkle with the breadcrumbs. Place the stuffed courgettes in a lightly greased ovenproof dish and bake in the oven at 220°C/425°F/gas mark 7 for 10 minutes until browned.

RAW COURGETTES WITH A VINAIGRETTE SAUCE

Serves 4

8 small courgettes, peeled and thinly sliced
salt and pepper
1 dessertspoon mustard
1 dessertspoon lemon juice
4 dessertspoons oil
1 dessertspoon chopped parsley

Place the sliced courgettes in a colander, sprinkle with salt and leave to stand for at

least 1 hour to extract the excess moisture. Meanwhile, make a vinaigrette; mix together the mustard, salt, pepper and lemon juice, then gradually add the oil. Arrange the courgettes in a serving dish and dress with the vinaigrette. Leave to stand for a short while, then sprinkle with the chopped parsley and serve.

SAUTÉED CELERY

Serves 4

1¹/₂ kg/3 lb celery
salt and pepper
2 dessertspoons flour
juice of ¹/₂ lemon
3 tbsp olive oil
2 garlic cloves, peeled and finely chopped

Trim off the leaves off the celery then chop the remainder into large pieces. Bring a pan of salted water to the boil. Mix the flour with enough cold water to make a thin paste and stir into the water. Add the celery and lemon juice, cover and cook until tender. Drain and set aside. Heat the oil in a large frying pan and sauté the chopped garlic for 2 minutes. Add the drained celery, season with pepper and cook briefly then serve.

Top: Raw Courgettes with a Vinaigrette Sauce
Bottom: Sautéd Celery

STEWED CHARD WITH PINE NUTS

Serves 4

1½kg/3lb chard
3 tomatoes, peeled and chopped
1 onion, peeled and finely chopped
2 garlic cloves, peeled and finely chopped
100 g/4 oz pine nuts
6 tbsp olive oil
salt

Cut the chard into large pieces and boil in salted water until just tender. Drain and set aside.
Heat the oil in a frying pan and sauté the garlic and onion until softened. Add the tomatoes, season with salt and cook for 10 minutes. Add the chard and the pine nuts and mix well. To finish, add 50 ml/2 fl oz boiling water and cook for a few more minutes.

LEEKS AU GRATIN

Serves 4

12 leeks
salt
100 g/4 oz Gruyère cheese, grated
50 g/2 oz butter

Wash the leeks, cut off the tops and root end and cook in boiling salted water until just tender. Drain the leeks and arrange in an ovenproof dish. Top with the grated cheese and melted butter then place in the oven at 220°C/425°F/gas mark 7 for a few minutes until browned.

CATALAN-STYLE SPINACH

Serves 4

1 kg/2.2 lb spinach, roughly chopped
100 g/4 oz pine nuts
100 g/4 oz raisins
100 g/4 oz butter

Cook the spinach in boiling salted water, drain and place in a heated serving dish. Heat the butter in a frying pan and sauté the pine nuts and the raisins. Pour over the spinach, stir and serve.

MALAGA-STYLE POTATOES

Serves 4

³/₄ kg/1½ lb potatoes, peeled and cubed
½ kg/1lb chard (sea kale), roughly chopped
salt
3 tbsp olive oil
2 garlic cloves, peeled and chopped

Cook the potatoes and chard together in boiling salted water until tender. Drain and set aside. Heat the oil in a large frying pan and sauté the garlic until it begins to turn golden. Add the chard and potatoes and cook for a few minutes over a high heat, stirring constantly, then serve.

Opposite, top: Stewed Chard with Pine Nuts
Opposite, bottom: Leeks au Gratin
Below, top: Catalan-style Spinach
Below, bottom: Malaga-style Potatoes

RATATOUILLE

Serves 4

2 aubergines, sliced
4 tbsp olive oil
2 onions, peeled and chopped
1 garlic clove, peeled and crushed
4 tomatoes, peeled and chopped
2 courgettes, sliced
salt and pepper
1 tbsp chopped parsley

Place the aubergine slices in a colander, sprinkle with salt and leave for 30 minutes to drain off the excess moisture. Rinse and dry the aubergines. Heat the oil in a frying pan and sauté the chopped onions, garlic and the tomatoes for a few minutes. Add the aubergines, courgettes and salt and pepper. Stir well and cook over a low heat for 30 minutes. Sprinkle with the parsley and serve hot or cold.

GREEN BEANS PROVENCAL

Serves 4

1 kg/2.2lb green beans
1/2 litre/3/4 pint fresh tomato sauce
1 tbsp chopped oregano
salt

Cook the beans in boiling, salted water until just tender, then drain. Heat the tomato sauce in a saucepan, add the beans and cook over a low heat for 15 minutes. Sprinkle with the oregano and serve.

SICILIAN-STYLE MUSHROOMS

Serves 4

4 tbsp olive oil
1 onion, peeled and chopped
1 garlic clove, peeled and chopped
1/2 kg/1 lb tomatoes, peeled and chopped
1/2 kg/1 lb mushrooms, chopped
100 ml/4 fl oz white wine
salt
1 tbsp chopped parsley

Heat the oil in a frying pan and sauté the chopped onion and garlic for 2 minutes.

Add the chopped tomatoes and cook for 15 minutes. Stir in the mushrooms and wine, season with salt and cook over a low heat until the sauce thickens. Sprinkle with the parsley and serve.

ANDALUSIAN-STYLE ASPARAGUS

Serves 4

4 tbsp olive oil
2 garlic cloves, peeled
1 slice bread
1 tbsp chopped parsley
1 kg/2.2 lb asparagus, roughly chopped
½ tsp paprika
1 tbsp wine vinegar
salt and pepper

Heat the oil in a frying pan and sauté the garlic until golden, then remove from the pan and set aside. Fry the bread and parsley in the same oil, remove and set aside. Add the asparagus and paprika to the pan, cook for 2 minutes, stirring, then cover and cook over a very low heat until the asparagus is just tender.

Meanwhile, mash the garlic and the bread with a pestle and mortar to form a paste. Dilute the paste with a little water. When the asparagus is cooked, pour over the garlic mixture and the vinegar. Season with salt and pepper and cook for a few more minutes.

Opposite: Ratatouille
Below: Green Beans Provencal

ARTICHOKES NICOISE

Serves 4

8 small artichokes
pared rind of 2 lemons
50 ml/2 fl oz oil
1 onion, peeled and chopped
1 kg/2.2 lb tomatoes, peeled and chopped
1 bouquet garni (thyme, bay leaf and parsley)
salt and pepper
80g/3¹/₂ oz breadcrumbs
25 g/1 oz butter

Remove the stalks, outer leaves and tips of the artichokes. Place in a large pan with just enough water to cover, add the lemon rind and salt and simmer for about 20 minutes until tender. Leave to cool, then drain and remove the hearts. Meanwhile, heat the oil in a saucepan and sauté the chopped onion for 2 minutes. Add the tomatoes and bouquet garni and cook over a low heat for 30 minutes. Taste and adjust the seasoning.
Spoon the tomato mixture into the artichoke bases and arrange them in a greased ovenproof dish. Top with the breadcrumbs and butter, and brown in the oven at 220°C/425°F/gas mark 7 for a few minutes.

AUBERGINES STUFFED WITH BROWN RICE

Serves 4

4 aubergines
3 tbsp olive oil
1 onion, peeled and chopped
2 tomatoes, peeled and chopped
1 tbsp chopped thyme and oregano
salt
170 g/6 oz cooked brown rice
100 g/4 oz Cheddar cheese, grated

Cut the aubergines in half lengthways and carefully scrape out the flesh. Heat the oil in a frying pan and sauté the onion for 2 minutes. Add the tomatoes, herbs and salt and cook for 15 minutes until soft. Chop the aubergine flesh and add to the pan, stir well and cook for a few minutes. Add the rice and mix together well. Place the aubergines in a greased ovenproof dish and stuff with the rice mixture. Sprinkle over the cheese and bake in the oven at 180°C/350°F/gas mark 4 for 30 minutes.

AUBERGINES WITH MINT

Serves 4

4 aubergines, sliced
1 garlic clove, peeled and chopped
1 tbsp chopped mint
8 tbsp virgin olive oil
2 tbsp sherry vinegar
salt

Cook the aubergines in boiling salted water until tender. Drain well and arrange in a serving dish. Dress the aubergines with the salt, oil, vinegar, chopped garlic and mint.

AUBERGINES WITH MOZZARELLA

Serves 4

³/₄ kg/1¹/₂ lb aubergines, sliced
salt
1 egg, beaten
4 tbsp flour
75 ml/3 fl oz olive oil
¹/₄ kg/¹/₂ lb Mozzarella cheese, sliced
300 ml/¹/₂ pint fresh tomato sauce

Place the aubergine slices in a colander, sprinkle with salt and leave for 30 minutes to draw out the bitter juices. Rinse and pat dry, then dip in beaten egg and flour. Heat the oil in a frying pan and fry the aubergines for 5 minutes, turning once. Arrange half the aubergines in a greased ovenproof dish. Place half the cheese slices on top and cover with half the tomato sauce. Repeat the layers once more, then bake in the oven at 220°C/425°F/gas mark 7 for 15 minutes or until the cheese has melted.

AUBERGINES WITH WALNUT SAUCE

Serves 4

4 aubergines, sliced
salt
5 tbsp flour
75 ml/3 fl oz olive oil
1 onion, peeled and chopped
2 garlic cloves, peeled and chopped
3 tomatoes, peeled and chopped
2 tbsp chopped parsley
6 walnuts, finely chopped

Soak the aubergine slices in salted, cold water for 30 minutes. Drain and dry well. Flour the aubergine slices and fry in the hot oil for 3 minutes, turning once.

Remove and set aside. Add the onion, garlic, tomatoes and parsley to the pan and cook for 5 minutes, stirring occasionally. Return the aubergines to the pan with the chopped walnuts. Mix together well and cook for 10 minutes.

CELERY IN BUTTER

Serves 4

1¹/₂ kg/3 lb celery
salt and pepper
2 tbsp flour
squeeze of lemon juice
50 g/2 oz butter
1 tbsp chopped parsley

Trim off the leaves and root of the celery, then chop the remainder into fairly large pieces. Bring a pan of salted water to the boil. Mix the flour with enough cold water to make a thin paste and stir into the water. Add the celery and a squeeze of lemon juice and cook until tender. Drain well, then return to the pan with the butter. Season with pepper, cover and heat for a few minutes. Serve sprinkled with the chopped parsley.

Top: Artichokes Niçoise
Bottom: Celery in Butter

SPANISH-STYLE GREEN BEANS

Serves 4

75 ml/3 fl oz olive oil
2 onions, peeled and finely sliced
1 garlic clove, peeled and chopped
¹/₄ kg/¹/₂ lb tomatoes, peeled and chopped
1 kg/2.2 lb green beans, roughly chopped
salt
1 tbsp chopped parsley

Heat the oil in a frying pan and sauté the onions for 2 minutes. Add the garlic, tomatoes and green beans. Season with salt and cook over a low heat until the beans are tender. Add the chopped parsley and serve immediately.

Top: Spanish-style Green Beans
Bottom: Stewed Broad Beans

STEWED BROAD BEANS

Serves 4

3 tbsp olive oil
2 onions, peeled and chopped
2 garlic cloves
³/₄ kg/1¹/₂ lb tomatoes, peeled and chopped
1 kg/2.2 lb shelled broad beans
1 bay leaf
1 tsp chopped thyme
pinch of grated nutmeg

100 ml/4 fl oz white wine
salt

Heat the oil in a frying pan and sauté the chopped onions for 2 minutes. Add the garlic and tomatoes and cook for 10 minutes. Add the broad beans, bay leaf, thyme, nutmeg, white wine and salt. Cover and cook over a low heat until the broad beans are tender.

PEPPERS STUFFED WITH RICE

Serves 4

3 tbsp olive oil
1 onion, peeled and finely chopped
200 g/7 oz rice
salt and pepper

Top: Asparagus with Cheese (recipe on page 36
Bottom: Peppers Stuffed with Rice

4 small green peppers, deseeded
knob of butter

Heat the oil in a frying pan and sauté the onion and rice for 2 minutes, stirring. Add twice the volume of water to the rice, season with salt and pepper and cook until the liquid is absorbed. Stuff the peppers with the rice mixture, then arrange in an ovenproof dish greased with butter. Bake in the oven at 180°C/350°F/gas mark 4 for 15 minutes.

ASPARAGUS WITH CHEESE

Serves 4

1 kg/2.2 lb asparagus
50 g/2 oz butter
4 egg yolks
100 g/4 oz Gruyère cheese, grated
white pepper
pinch of grated nutmeg
salt

Cook the asparagus in a large pan of simmering, salted water for 20-30 minutes until tender. Drain well and arrange in a serving dish.
Melt the butter in a mixing bowl placed over a pan of simmering water. Add the egg yolks and mix well. Stir in the cheese, pepper, nutmeg, salt and cream. Pour the sauce over the asparagus and serve immediately, garnished with extra grated cheese, if desired.

VEGETABLES AU GRATIN

Serves 4

8 eggs
4 dessertspoons single cream
200 g/7 oz Cheddar cheese, grated
salt and pepper
punch of nutmeg
knob of butter
3 courgettes, sliced
4 tomatoes, quartered
1 green pepper, deseeded, sliced into rings
1 red pepper, deseeded, sliced into rings

Place the eggs and cream in a mixing bowl with half the grated cheese and beat well together. Season with salt, pepper and nutmeg and pour the mixture into an ovenproof dish greased with butter. Add the vegetables to the egg mixture and bake in the oven at 220°C/425°F/gas mark 7 for 30 minutes. Sprinkle with the remaining cheese and return to the oven for 15 minutes.

AUBERGINES WITH TOMATO SAUCE

Serves 4

4 medium-sized aubergines, peeled and finely sliced
salt
75 ml/3 fl oz olive oil
1/4 litre/7 fl oz tomato sauce
50 g/2 oz Gruyère cheese, grated
1 tbsp chopped parsley

Place the aubergine slices in a colander, sprinkle with salt and leave to drain for 1 hour to extract the bitter juices. Rinse and dry well. Heat the oil in a frying pan and fry the aubergines for 10 minutes, turning once. Arrange in an ovenproof dish with alternate layers of the tomato sauce. Top with the grated cheese and brown in the oven at 220°C/425°F/gas mark 7 for about 15 minutes. Serve immediately, topped with the parsley.

FRIED COURGETTES WITH TOMATO AND GREEN PEPPER SAUCE

Serves 6

100 ml/4 fl oz olive oil
1/2 kg/1 lb onions, peeled and chopped
1/2 kg/1 lb green peppers, deseeded and chopped
3/4 kg/1 1/2 lb courgettes, peeled and chopped
salt

Heat the oil in a frying pan and sauté the chopped onions over a low heat for 2 minutes. Add the chopped peppers and cook for a few minutes, stirring well. Add the chopped tomatoes and cook over a low heat until the vegetables are tender. Meanwhile, quickly fry the cubed courgettes over a high heat. Add the courgettes to the sauce, season, mix well and serve.

CHARD AU GRATIN

Serves 4

1 kg/2.2 lb chard (sea kale), roughly chopped
3 tbsp olive oil
2 garlic cloves, peeled and chopped
2 tbsp chopped parsley
100 g/4 oz pine nuts
100 g/4 oz breadcrumbs
salt and pepper
100 g/4 oz Cheddar cheese, grated
75 g/3 oz butter, melted

Cook the chard in boiling salted water until just tender. Drain and set aside. Heat the oil in a frying pan and sauté the chopped garlic with the parsley, pine nuts and half the breadcrumbs for 3 minutes. Add the chard and mix well. Season and turn the mixture into an ovenproof dish greased with butter. Top with the remaining breadcrumbs, the grated cheese and the melted butter. Brown in the oven at 220°C/425°F/gas mark 7 for 10 minutes.

LEEK PIE

Serves 4

250 g/8 oz shortcrust pastry
3 egg yolks
3 tbsp single cream
salt and pepper
1/2 kg/1 lb leeks, cooked and cut into thin slices

Roll out the pastry and use to line a medium-sized quiche tin or 4 individual flan tins. Beat the egg yolks with the cream and season with salt and pepper. Mix in the chopped, cooked leeks and pour into the pastry case(s). Bake in the oven at 190°C/375°F/gas mark 5 for 25-30 minutes until golden brown on top.

Top: Chard au Gratin
Bottom: Leek Pie

TOMATOES STUFFED WITH AVOCADO

Serves 4

8 tomatoes
1 avocado
squeeze of lemon juice
200 g/7 oz cottage cheese
1 tbsp chopped chives
salt and pepper

Cut the tomatoes in half horizontally. Scoop out the flesh carefully and leave the tomato halves to stand upside-down for 30 minutes. Halve the avocado, remove the stone and scoop out the flesh into a mixing bowl. Sprinkle with lemon juice and mash with a fork to make a paste. Stir in the cottage cheese and chives and season with salt and pepper. Fill the tomatoes with the avocado mixture and serve, garnished with slivers of cheese, if desired.

CAULIFLOWER AU GRATIN

Serves 4

1 cauliflower
salt and pepper
4 potatoes, peeled and chopped
75 g/3 oz butter
50 g/2 oz flour
1/4 litre/7 fl oz milk
100 g/4 oz Gruyère cheese, grated

Cook the potatoes in boiling, salted water. Break the cauliflower into florets and cook in boiling, salted water until tender. Drain and reserve 1/4 litre/7 fl oz of the cooking liquid. Heat most of the butter in a saucepan, stir in the flour and cook until just changing colour. Add the reserved cooking liquid and the milk, season with pepper and cook over a low heat for 10 minutes, stirring occasionally. Grease an ovenproof dish with the remaining butter. Place the cauliflower and potatoes in the dish, stir half the cheese into the sauce and pour over. Top with the remaining cheese and brown in the oven at 220°C/425°F/gas mark 7 for 10 minutes.

Left: Tomatoes Stuffed with Avocado
Right: Cauliflower au Gratin

TOMATOES WITH APPLE SAUCE

Serves 4

4 tomatoes
3 apples, peeled and grated
100 g/4 oz mixed walnuts and almonds,
finely chopped
2 tbsp mayonnaise
4 lettuce leaves

Slice the tops off the tomatoes and scoop out the flesh. Mix together the grated apples and nuts and fill the tomato shells.

Top with the mayonnaise and serve on a bed of lettuce.

RED CABBAGE WITH APPLES

Serves 4

100 g/4 oz butter
1 medium-sized red cabbage, shredded
2 Cox's orange pippin apples, peeled and
chopped
1 tsp cider vinegar
75 ml/3 fl oz water
salt
1 tsp sugar

Grease a flameproof casserole dish with a little of the butter. Add the cabbage, apples, vinegar and water, season and mix well together. Cover and cook over a low heat for 40 minutes. Stir well and serve immediately.

COUNTRY-STYLE POTATOES

Serves 4

4 tbsp olive oil
2 onions, peeled and sliced
3/4 kg/1 1/2 lb potatoes, peeled and chopped
1 bay leaf
1 tbsp chopped mixed thyme and mint
salt
225 ml/8 fl oz boiling water

Heat the oil in a large frying pan and sauté the onions for 5 minutes. Add the remaining ingredients, cook over a low heat for 20 minutes and serve.

GENOA AUGERGINES

Serves 4

4 aubergines, sliced
4 tbsp olive oil
1 onion, peeled and chopped
2 tomatoes, peeled and chopped
salt and pepper
2 eggs, beaten

Soak the aubergine slices in cold water for 30 minutes. Drain and pat dry. Heat the olive oil in a large frying pan and sauté the onions for 5 minutes. Add the aubergines, tomatoes and salt and pepper. Cover and cook for 20 minutes until the vegetables are tender. Pour over the beaten eggs, mix well and serve immediately.

Left, top: Tomatoes with Apple Sauce
Left, bottom: Genoa Aubergines
Right, top: Red Cabbage with Apples
Right, bottom: Country-style Potatoes

COURGETTES WITH GRUYERE CHEESE

Serves 4

4 courgettes
100 g/4 oz Gruyère cheese, grated
3 eggs, beaten
3 tbsp fresh tomato sauce
75 g/3 oz breadcrumbs
150 ml/^{1}/$_4$ pint olive oil
salt

Parboil the courgettes in salted water. Drain, cut in half lengthways and scoop out the flesh. Mash the courgette flesh with the grated cheese and the tomato sauce. Stuff the courgettes with this mixture, coat in beaten egg and breadcrumbs and fry in the hot oil.

CAULIFLOWER WITH AVOCADO

Serves 4

1 cauliflower
4 avocados
100 g/4 oz almonds, finely chopped
3 tbsp olive oil
1 tbsp wine vinegar
small bunch of radishes
salt and pepper

Divide the cauliflower into florets and cook in boiling, salted water until just tender. Drain and leave to cool, then place in a serving dish. Mix together the oil and vinegar, season and pour over the cauliflower. Mash the avocado flesh with the almonds and season with salt and pepper.

Cover the cauliflower with this paste and decorate with the radishes.

Left: Courgettes with Gruyère Cheese
Right: Cauliflower with Avocado

MIXED VEGETABLE CASSEROLE

Serves 4

1 aubergine, sliced
4 tbsp olive oil
1 onion, peeled and sliced
1 green pepper, deseeded and sliced
150 g/5 oz mushrooms, chopped
2 tomatoes, chopped
1 tsp chopped mixed herbs (basil, oregano and thyme)
salt and black pepper

Place the aubergine slices in a colander, sprinkle with salt and leave to drain for 30 minutes. Rinse and dry well. Heat the oil in a flameproof casserole dish and gently fry the onion and pepper for 2 minutes. Add the aubergine, mushrooms, tomatoes, herbs, salt and pepper. Stir well, cover and cook over a low heat for about 30 minutes until the vegetables are tender. Serve hot.

TOMATOES PROVENÇAL

Serves 4

6 tomatoes
2 tbsp olive oil
2 small onions, peeled and finely chopped
50 g/2 oz butter
50 g/2 oz grated Parmesan cheese

Slice the tops off four of the tomatoes and carefully remove the flesh. Chop the remaining tomatoes. Heat the oil in a frying pan and gently fry the onion and chopped tomatoes until softened. Stuff the hollowed out tomatoes with this mixture, top with knobs of butter, sprinkle with grated cheese and bake in the oven at 200°C/400°F/gas mark 6 for 15 minutes.

PEAS WITH MINT

Serves 4

100 g/4 oz butter
1 lettuce, shredded
14 spring onions, chopped
1 tsp sugar
1 tbsp chopped mint
salt and pepper
1 kg/2.2 lb peas

Heat the butter in a flameproof casserole dish, add the shredded lettuce, spring onions, sugar and mint. Season with salt and pepper and sauté for a few minutes. Add the peas, cover and cook over a low heat until the peas are tender. Serve

immediately, garnished with cooked spring onions (white part of the onion only) if desired.

Right, top: Mixed Vegetable Casserole
Right, bottom: Tomatoes Provençal
Opposite, top: Peas with Mint
Opposite, bottom: Greek-style Mushrooms

GREEK-STYLE MUSHROOMS

Serves 4

1/2 kg/1 lb mushrooms, sliced
juice of 1 lemon
3 tbsp olive oil
1 dessertspoon coriander seeds
salt and pepper

Heat the oil in a frying pan and sauté the mushrooms briefly. Add the lemon juice and coriander seeds, season with salt and pepper and cook over a high heat for 8 minutes. Serve cold.

POTATOES AU GRATIN

Serves 4

1 kg/2.2 lb potatoes, peeled and thinly sliced
salt and pepper
1/4 litre/7 fl oz single cream
50 g/2 oz Cheddar cheese, grated
1 tbsp chopped parsley
50 g/2 oz butter

Arrange the potatoes in layers in a lightly greased roasting tin. Season with salt and pepper. Mix the cream with the grated cheese and chopped parsley. Pour over the potatoes and top with knobs of butter. Bake in the oven at 180°C/350°F/gas mark 4 for 30 minutes until golden brown.

CELERY WITH PINE NUTS

Serves 4

1 kg/2.2 lb celery, chopped
75 g/3 oz butter
50 g/2 oz pine nuts
100 ml/4 fl oz vegetable stock
50 ml/2 fl oz single cream
salt and pepper

Heat most of the butter in a frying pan and sauté the celery for 2 minutes. Add the stock, season with salt and pepper and cook over a low heat for 15 minutes. Add the cream and cook for a further 10 minutes. Meanwhile, heat the remaining butter in a small frying pan and brown the pine nuts. Sprinkle the pine nuts over the cooked celery and serve.

CARROT AND CHEESE FLAN

Serves 4

500 g/1 lb carrots, peeled and sliced
250 g/8 oz cream cheese
1 dessertspoon chopped chives
1 dessertspoon chopped parsley
salt and white pepper

Cook the carrots in boiling, salted water until tender. Drain and liquidise in a blender or food processor. Allow to cool, then add the remaining ingredients and stir well together. Pour the mixture into a non-stick mould and refrigerate for about 3 hours before serving.

SPANISH-STYLE ARTICHOKES

Serves 4

8 small artichokes
1 tbsp olive oil
1 onion, peeled and finely chopped
2 tbsp flour
100 ml/4 fl oz white wine
100 ml/4 fl oz vegetable stock
salt and pepper
50 ml/2 fl oz single cream

Remove the stalks, outer leaves and the tips of the artichokes. Cook in boiling, salted water for about 30 minutes until tender. Drain and set aside.

Meanwhile, heat the oil in a flameproof casserole and sauté the onion until soft. Add the flour and stir well. Cut the artichokes into quarters then add to the onion with the wine and vegetable stock and season with salt and pepper. Cook over a low heat, stirring occasionally, until the sauce thickens. Stir in the cream, heat through and serve hot.

CAULIFLOWER WITH MUSHROOMS

Serves 4

1 cauliflower, divided into florets
1 onion, peeled and chopped
2 tomatoes, peeled and chopped
150 g/6oz mushrooms, chopped
1 garlic clove, peeled and chopped
1 tbsp chopped parsley
salt
2 tbsp olive oil

Cook the cauliflower florets in boiling, salted water until just tender. Drain and set aside. Heat the oil in a frying pan and sauté the chopped onion and garlic for a few minutes then add the mushrooms, tomatoes, parsley and salt and cook for 5 minutes. Place the cauliflower in a heated serving dish and pour over the sauce. Serve garnished with chopped parsley.

STEWED ARTICHOKES

Serves 6

12 small artichokes
100 ml/4 fl oz oil
1 medium-sized onion, peeled and finely chopped
3 garlic cloves, peeled and finely chopped
100 ml/4 fl oz white wine
pinch of grated nutmeg

Remove the outer leaves from the artichokes then cut each artichoke into quarters. Heat the oil in a large, flameproof casserole dish and sauté the artichokes for 2 minutes. Add the onion and garlic and cook until softened. Add the wine and nutmeg, season, cover and cook over a low heat for 20 minutes until the artichokes are tender. If necessary, add a little water to prevent the mixture from drying out.

RED CABBAGE CASSEROLE

Serves 6

1 large red cabbage, finely sliced
100 ml/4 fl oz oil
2 onions, peeled and sliced
3 garlic cloves, peeled and chopped
1 bay leaf
dash of wine vinegar
salt and pepper

Place all the ingredients in a flameproof casserole dish. Pour in just enough water to cover the cabbage, cover and cook over a very low heat for about 40 minutes until the cabbage is soft and most of the liquid has evaporated.

Top: Spanish-style Artichokes
Bottom: Cauliflower with Musrooms

RICE AND PASTA

NOODLES WITH AUBERGINES

Serves 4

100 ml/4 fl oz olive oil
1 onion, peeled and sliced
3 tomatoes, peeled and chopped
1 tbsp chopped basil
salt and pepper
3 aubergines, sliced
40 g/1½ oz grated Parmesan cheese
350 g/12 oz noodles

Heat half the oil in a frying pan and sauté the onion for 2 minutes. Add the chopped tomatoes and basil. Season and cook over a low heat for 40 minutes.

Heat the remaining oil in another frying pan and fry the aubergine slices for 10 minutes, turning once. Cook the noodles in boiling, salted water, drain well and place in a heated serving dish. Add the tomato sauce, top with the fried aubergines and sprinkle with the grated cheese.

SPINACH LASAGNE

Serves 4

50 g/2 oz butter
350 g/12 oz spinach, cooked, drained and chopped
25 g/1 oz raisins
25 g/1 oz pine nuts
salt and pepper
pinch of grated nutmeg
½ litre/¾ pint béchamel sauce
170 g/6 oz lasagne verde
100 g/4 oz Cheddar cheese, grated

Heat the butter in a saucepan, add the spinach, raisins and pine nuts and cook, stirring, for 2 minutes. Season with salt, pepper and nutmeg and mix in a little béchamel sauce. Pour a little béchamel sauce into an ovenproof dish greased with butter, and arrange a layer of lasgne on top. Top the lasagne with a layer of the spinach mixture, cover with a little more sauce and arrange another layer of lasagne on top. Top with more béchamel and grated cheese. Repeat until all the lasagne is used up. Finally, top with béchamel sauce, sprinkle with grated cheese and bake in the oven at 190°C/375°F/gas

mark 5 for 30 minutes.

NOODLES WITH MOZZARELLA CHEESE

Serves 4

5 tbsp olive oil
3 tomatoes, peeled and chopped
100 g/4 oz Mozzarella cheese, cubed
50 g/2 oz mild hard cheese, grated
1 tsp chopped oregano
salt and pepper
350 g/12 oz noodles

Heat the oil in a saucepan and add the tomatoes, the Mozzarella, the grated cheese, the oregano, salt and pepper. Cover and cook slowly for 30 minutes.

Meanwhile, cook the noodles in boiling, salted water, drain and place in an oven-proof dish. Mix with the cheese mixture and place in the oven at 200°C/400°F/gas mark 6 for 10 minutes. Serve immediately.

ARGENTINIAN RICE

Serves 4

4 tbsp olive oil
1 onion, peeled and chopped
2 garlic cloves, peeled and chopped
1 tomato, peeled and chopped
1 tbsp chopped parsley
1 litre/1¾ pints water
300 g/10 oz rice
salt
300 ml/½ pint fresh tomato sauce
50 g/2 oz Cheddar cheese, grated

Heat half the oil in a saucepan and lightly sauté the chopped onion and garlic. Add the chopped tomatoes, parsley and water and cook for 15 minutes. In a separate pan, fry the rice in the remaining oil until golden, add the vegetable mixture, season and add a little more water. Simmer for 30 minutes until the rice is cooked. Pour the mixture into a greased soufflé dish or individual ramekins and bake in the oven at 190°C/375°F/gas mark 5 for 15 minutes. Turn out onto a serving dish and top with the tomato sauce and grated cheese.

THREE DELIGHT RICE

Serves 4

300 g/10 oz rice
4 tbsp olive oil
1 onion, peeled and finely chopped
1 carrot, peeled and finely chopped
1 green pepper, deseeded and finely chopped
150 g/5 oz mushrooms, finely chopped
100 g/4 oz peas, cooked
2 garlic cloves, peeled and finely chopped
1 egg, beaten
salt
3 sprigs parsley

Cook the rice in boiling, salted water until tender. Drain and reserve. Heat the oil in a large frying pan, add the vegetables and fry, stirring, for 10 minutes until softened. Add the rice and beaten egg, season and stir for a few minutes over a high heat. Leave to stand for a few minutes then serve garnished with parsley sprigs.

MILANESE RICE

Serves 4

250 g/8 oz rice
½ litre/¾ pint vegetable stock
50 g/2 oz butter
1 onion, peeled and finely chopped
100 g/4 oz Gruyère cheese, grated
pinch of powdered saffron
salt and pepper

Heat the butter in a frying pan and sauté the chopped onion for 2 minutes. Add the rice, sauté for a few minutes then add the stock. Season with the salt, pepper and saffron. Cover and cook for 20 minutes until the rice is tender. Remove the pan from the heat and add the cheese. Mix well and serve immediately.

Top: Argentinian Rice
Bottom: Three Delight Rice

PASTA WITH HAZELNUTS

Serves 4

3 tbsp olive oil
200 g/7 oz carrots, peeled and finely sliced
1 medium-sized onion, peeled and finely
chopped
75 ml/3 fl oz white wine
200 g/7 oz cottage cheese
1 tbsp chopped parsley
salt
350 g/12 oz spaghetti or tagliatelle
75 g/3 oz hazelnuts, chopped

Heat the oil in a frying pan and fry the carrots and onion for 5 minutes. Add the wine, cottage cheese, chopped parsley and salt. Heat together gently over a low heat.
   Meanwhile, cook the pasta in boiling, salted water until "al dente". Drain well and place in a heated serving dish. Pour over the sauce and top with the hazelnuts.

VEGETARIAN PAELLA

Serves 4

3 tbsp olive oil
1 onion, peeled and finely chopped
2 garlic cloves, peeled and finely chopped
200 g/7 oz rice
2 tomatoes, peeled and finely chopped
salt
100 /4 oz peas
100 g/4 oz broad beans
few strands of saffron
2 small green peppers, finely sliced

Heat the oil in a large frying pan or paella pan. Fry the onion and garlic for 2 minutes, then add the tomatoes and cook for a few more minutes. Add the rice, salt and saffron strands. Mix well and add water (approximately double the amount of the rice). Cook over a low heat until the rice is tender. Towards the end of the cooking time, add the peppers, peas and broad beans. Leave to stand for a few minutes then serve garnished with chopped parsley and slivers of cheese, if desired.

Left: Pasta with Hazelnuts
Right: Vegetarian Paella

KITCHEN GARDEN SPAGHETTI

Serves 4

350 g/12 oz spaghetti
2 carrots, peeled and finely chopped
2 leeks, finely chopped
1 celery stalk, finely chopped
6 tbsp olive oil
25 g/1 oz butter
salt and pepper
75 g/3 oz Gruyère cheese, grated

Heat the oil in a frying pan, add all the vegetables and cook, stirring for 2 minutes. Season with salt and pepper, cover and cook slowly for 30 minutes, adding a little water if necessary, to prevent the vegetables from sticking.

Cook the spaghetti in boiling, salted water, drain and place in a saucepan with the butter. Mix well. Add the fried vegetables and the cheese and serve.

VEGETABLE AND ALMOND MACARONI

Serves 4

1/4 kg/1/2 lb macaroni
3 tbsp oil
1 onion, peeled and finely chopped
200 g/7 oz mushrooms, finely chopped
2 tomatoes, peeled and chopped
salt
200 g/7 oz peas, cooked
75 g/3 oz almonds, toasted
100 g/4 oz butter, melted
50 g/2 oz Cheddar cheese, grated

Cook the macaroni in boiling, salted water. Drain, rinse in cold water and drain again.

Meanwhile, heat the oil in a frying pan and fry the onion and mushrooms for 2 minutes. Add the tomatoes and cook for a few more minutes. Season with salt, add the peas and continue cooking for a few more minutes. Remove the pan from the heat and add the almonds.

Place half the macaroni in an ovenproof serving dish and top with the fried vegetables. Add the remaining macaroni, pour over the melted butter and sprinkle on the grated cheese. Brown in the oven at 220°C/425°F/gas mark 7 for a few minutes before serving.

MACARONI CAPUCHIN

Serves 4

5 tbsp olive oil
1 onion, peeled and finely chopped
1 small cauliflower, divided into florets, cooked
50 g/2 oz raisins
50 g/2 oz pine nuts
pinch of powdered saffron
salt and pepper
300 g/10 oz macaroni

Heat the oil in a large saucepan and sauté the onion for 2 minutes. Add the cooked cauliflower florets, raisins, pine nuts, saffron, salt and pepper and cook over a low heat.

Meanwhile, cook the macaroni in boiling, salted water, drain and add to the vegetables. Mix well and serve immediately.

RICE WITH SPINACH

Serves 4

50 ml/2 fl oz oil
2 garlic cloves, peeled and sliced
3/4 kg/1 1/2 lb spinach, chopped
1/4 kg/1/2 lb rice
salt and pepper
50 g/2 oz Gruyère cheese, grated
1 tbsp chopped parsley

Heat half the oil in a frying pan and gently fry half the garlic until soft but not coloured. Add the chopped spinach and cook over a low heat until the juices have evaporated.

Meanwhile, cook the rice in plenty of boiling, salted water for 20 minutes until tender. Drain well and set aside.

Heat the remaining oil in another frying pan, fry the remaining garlic for 2 minutes then add the rice and cook, stirring for 3 minutes. Stir in the spinach, season with salt and pepper, sprinkle with the cheese and parsley and serve.

TAGLIATELLE WITH MUSHROOMS

Serves 4

1/4 kg/1/2 lb tagliatelle
4 tbsp olive oil
1/2 kg/1 lb mushrooms, sliced
juice of 1 lemon
3 tbsp chopped parsley
salt

Cook the tagliatelle in boiling, salted water. Drain and set aside. Heat the oil in a large saucepan, add the mushrooms, lemon juice, parsley and salt and cook over a low heat for 15 minutes. Add the pasta, mix well and heat for a few more minutes.

PASTA BOWS WITH COURGETTES

Serves 4

5 tbsp olive oil
1 onion, peeled and finely chopped
1 tbsp chopped basil
4 medium-sized courgettes, peeled and sliced
salt and white pepper
3 tomatoes, peeled and chopped
400 g/14 oz pasta bows (farfalle)
50 g/2 oz grated Parmesan cheese

Heat the oil in a frying pan and lightly sauté the chopped onion and basil. Add the courgettes, season with salt and pepper and cook over a low heat for a few minutes. Add the tomatoes, cover and cook over a low heat for 20 minutes.

Cook the pasta bows in boiling, salted water, drain and place in a heated serving dish. Pour over the sauce, sprinkle with the cheese and serve immediately.

ORIENTAL RICE

Serves 4

300 g/10 oz brown rice, cooked
2 eggs, beaten
2 onions, peeled and finely chopped
2 garlic cloves, peeled and finely chopped
3 tbsp olive oil
soya sauce
pinch of grated nutmeg
pinch of ground ginger
salt

Heat the oil in a frying pan, add the onion and garlic and cook for 5 minutes until softened. Stir in the remaining ingredients, heat through thoroughly, and serve.

Top: Pasta Bows with Courgettes
Bottom: Oriental Rice

SPAGHETTI WITH PESTO SAUCE

Serves 4

25 g/1oz basil leaves
2 garlic cloves, peeled and roughly chopped
pinch of salt
50 g/2 oz grated goat's cheese
40 g/1½ oz grated Parmesan cheese
100 ml/4 fl oz oil
400 g/14 oz spaghetti

Using a pestle and mortar, pound together the basil, garlic and salt. Gradually add half the goat's cheese and all the Parmesan and mash together well. Gradually add the oil, stirring constantly. Cook the spaghetti in boiling salted water, drain and sprinkle with the remaining goat's cheese. Stir in the basil sauce and serve immediately.

Spaghetti with Pesto Sauce

EGGS

EGG AND MUSHROOM RAMEKINS

Serves 4

50 g/2 oz butter

300 g/10 oz mushrooms, chopped
salt
4 eggs, beaten
50 g/2 oz Cheddar cheese, grated

Heat the butter in a saucepan and sauté the

Top: Egg and Mushroom Ramekins
Bottom: Country-style Omelette
(recipe on page 57)

mushrooms until tender. Season and stir in the beaten eggs. Cook until lightly scrambled then pour the mixture into individual ramekin dishes. Sprinkle with the grated cheese and serve hot.

COUNTRY-STYLE OMELETTE

Serves 4

4 tbsp olive oil
potatoes, peeled and cubed
1 onion, peeled and chopped
tomatoes, peeled and chopped
100 g/4 oz peas, cooked
150 g/6 oz green beans, cooked
1 carrot, peeled and sliced
salt and pepper
8 eggs, beaten

Heat the oil in a large frying pan and fry the potatoes and onion until almost cooked. Add the tomatoes and cook until softened. Add the peas, green beans and carrot, season with salt and pepper and sauté together for a few minutes. Pour in the beaten eggs, stir, then allow the omelette to set on the underside. As soon as it is set, place under a preheated hot grill until the top is golden brown.

EGG AND POTATO CASSEROLE

Serves 4

4 hard-boiled eggs, quartered
flour
olive oil
1/2 kg/1 lb potatoes, peeled and sliced
1 onion, peeled and chopped
50 ml/2 fl oz white wine
salt

Coat the quartered eggs in flour and fry in plenty of hot oil. Dip the sliced potatoes in flour and fry in the same hot oil. Place the eggs and potatoes in a flameproof casserole dish.

In a separate frying pan heat 2 tbsp of oil and sauté the chopped onion until softened. Add a teaspoon of flour, stirring well. Add the white wine and salt and cook over a low heat for a few minutes. Purée the mixture, then pour over the eggs and potatoes in the dish. Cover and cook over a low heat for 15 minutes.

Top: Eggs with Pepper Sauce
Bottom: Scrambled Eggs with Spring Onions

EGGS WITH PEPPER SAUCE

Serves 4

2 red peppers
225 ml/8 fl oz single cream
salt
50 g/ 2oz butter
4 eggs
50 g/2 oz grated Parmesan cheese

Grill the peppers until the skins are blistered and blackened. Allow to cool, then peel off the skin and purée the flesh. Mix the purée with the cream and salt. Grease an ovenproof dish with the butter, pour in the pepper sauce and break the eggs onto the surface. Sprinkle over the cheese and bake in the oven at 180°C/350°F/gas mark 4 for 10-15 minutes until the eggs are set.

WHEATGERM OMELETTE

Serves 4

1/2 onion, peeled and finely chopped
4 dessertspoons wheatgerm
4 eggs, beaten
salt
3 tbsp olive oil

Mix together the onion, wheatgerm and eggs. Season well. Heat the oil in a frying pan and pour in the egg mixture. Cook until set on the underside then turn the omelette over. As soon as the other side is set, serve immediately.

SCRAMBLED EGGS WITH SPRING ONIONS

Serves 4

1 bunch spring onions
8 eggs
50 g/2 oz butter
4 tbsp olive oil
salt and pepper

Wash the spring onions and remove the outer layers and the green parts. Slice them thinly. Sauté the garlic in oil, taking care not to let it burn. Sauté the spring onion briefly in the same oil. Beat the eggs, season with salt and pepper and add the butter (softened) and the garlic and spring onions, drained of oil. Put the mixture in a pan in a bain-marie and cook slowly, stirring constantly, until it acquires a thick, creamy consistency. Serve hot on pieces of fried bread.

HARD-BOILED EGGS WITH ROQUEFORT SAUCE

Serves 4

3 tbsp virgin olive oil
1 tbsp sherry vinegar
1 small onion, peeled and finely grated
1 tsp chopped parsley
200 g/7 oz Roquefort cheese
1/4 litre/7 fl oz single cream
salt
12 hard-boiled eggs, sliced
4 sprigs parsley

Make a vinaigrette with the oil, vinegar, onion and parsley. In a separate bowl, mash the cheese and gradually add the vinaigrette. Add the cream and beat the mixture until the sauce becomes creamy. Season. Arrange the slices of hard-boiled egg on a serving dish, pour over the cheese sauce and garnish with sprigs of parsley. Chill before serving.

BAKED EGGS

Serves 4

50 g/2 oz butter
1 small onion, peeled and chopped
salt
150 g/6 oz mushrooms, sliced
8 eggs
2 tsp chopped parsley

Heat half the butter in a frying pan and sauté the chopped onion until soft. Season and add the mushrooms, then cook until their juices have evaporated.

Divide the mixture between 4 individual ramekin dishes and break 2 eggs on top of each dish. Top with the remaining butter and place the ramekins in a roasting tin half-filled with hot water. Bake in the oven at 180°C/350°F/gas mark 4 for 10-15 minutes until the egg whites are set but the yolks still runny. Garnish with the chopped parsley and serve immediately.

DESSERTS

STRAWBERRY MOUSSE

Serves 4

1/2 kg/1 lb strawberries, hulled
3 eggs, beaten
2 egg yolks
75 g/3 oz sugar
15 g/1/2 oz gelatine
3 dessertspoons water
150 ml/1/4 pint double or whipping cream

Purée the strawberries in a blender or food processor. Put the eggs, egg yolks and sugar in a mixing bowl and place over a pan of simmering water. Cook, stirring constantly, until the mixture becomes creamy. Remove from the heat. Soak the gelatine in a saucepan with the water for about 5 minutes. Dissolve over a low heat without stirring. Allow to cool.

Mix the strawberry purée with the egg mixture and gradually add the cooled gelatine, stirring constantly. Fold in the whipped cream and leave to cool until nearly set, stirring occasionally. Pour the mousse into individual glasses and chill for 1 1/2 hours. Remove from the refrigerator 30 minutes before serving and garnish with whole strawberries.

TRADITIONAL APPLE PURÉE

Serves 4

4 ripe Cox's Orange Pippin apples
grated rind and juice of 1/2 lemon
100 g/4 oz demerara or granulated sugar
pinch of cinnamon

Peel, core and slice the apples. Place in a saucepan with a little water and the lemon juice. Simmer until tender then beat to a purée. Add the sugar and heat gently until the sugar is dissolved. Add the cinnamon and grated lemon rind. This purée may be served hot or cold.

KIWI SORBET

Serves 4

6 kiwi fruit (Chinese gooseberries), peeled and sliced
400 g/14 oz sugar
1 litre/1 3/4 pints water

juice of 1 lemon

Place the sugar and water in a saucepan and heat gently until the sugar is dissolved. Add the lemon juice, bring to the boil and simmer until the mixture is syrupy. Place the kiwi fruit in a liquidiser or food processor with the syrup and blend to a purée. Pour into a container, cover and freeze until semi-frozen. Turn into a bowl and beat with an electric whisk. Pour back into the container, cover and freeze until hard. Serve in individual dishes or in the empty shells of the kiwi fruit.

PUMPKIN PIE

Serves 4

1 kg/2.2 lb pumpkin, peeled and cubed
salt
4 eggs
1/4 litre/7 fl oz milk
1/4 kg/1/2 lb sugar
50 g/2 oz flour
5 dessertspoons single cream
50 g/2 oz currants, soaked in hot water
grated rind of 1 lemon
pinch of nutmeg
pinch of cinnamon
25 g/1 oz butter

Cook the cubed pumpkin in boiling salted water for 10 minutes. Drain well then mash thoroughly. Place the mashed pumpkin in a muslin-lined sieve and leave to drain for 2 hours.

Beat the eggs with the milk, sugar, flour and cream. Add the pumpkin purée and the drained, soaked currants. Flavour the mixture with the lemon rind, nutmeg and cinnamon. Pour the mixture into a flan dish greased with butter and cook in a bain-marie in the oven at 190°C/375°F/gas mark 5 for 40 minutes. Leave to cool and serve.

VANILLA RICE CAKE

Serves 4

200 g/7 oz long-grain rice
3/4 litre/1 1/2 pints milk
150 g/5 oz sugar
1 vanilla pod
salt

25 g/1 oz butter
5 egg yolks

Wash the rice in cold water. Place in a saucepan with enough cold water to cover, bring to the boil and cook for 6 minutes. Drain well. Place the milk and sugar in an ovenproof casserole dish and bring to boiling point. Add the rice, vanilla pod and a pinch of salt. When the mixture begins to boil again, add the butter, cover and cook in the oven at 180°C/350°F/gas mark 4 for 30 minutes.

Remove from the oven and blend in the egg yolks. Turn the mixture into 4 individual dishes or one large dish greased with butter. Chill for 2 hours before serving. Decorate with a dusting of cocoa powder and sliced fresh fruit, if desired.

AVOCADO DESSERT

Serves 4

4 ripe avocados
3 tbsp icing sugar
1/2 litre/3/4 pint double or whipping cream
50 ml/2 fl oz cognac

Cut the avocados in half lengthways and remove the stones. Scoop out the flesh, taking care not to break the skins. Mash the avocado flesh to a purée with the sugar and cognac. Add the whipped cream and mix well. Fill the avocado skins with the purée and chill for 2 hours before serving. Decorate with fesh fruit and extra whipped cream, if desired.

Top: Vanilla Rice Cake
Bottom: Avocado Dessert

PEARS WITH RAISINS

Serves 4

50 g/2 oz seedless raisins
100 ml/4 fl oz sweet sherry
250 g/8 oz sugar
4 pears, halved, peeled and cored
1 cinnamon stick

Soak the raisins in the sweet sherry. Meanwhile, place the sugar in a large flameproof casserole with ³/4 litre/1¹/2 pints water. Bring to the boil and simmer until it becomes a light syrup. Add the pears and cinnamon to the syrup and simmer for about 12 minutes until the pears are tender. Carefully remove the pears from the syrup, arrange in a serving dish and leave to cool. Reduce the syrup over a high heat for 5 minutes. Pour the syrup and then the raisins soaked in sherry over the pears. Serve cold.

BANANAS IN CREAM

Serves 4

6 bananas
juice of 1 lemon
75 g/3 oz butter
1 dessertspoon sugar
50 ml/2 fl oz rum
100 ml/4 fl oz single cream
50 g/2 oz almonds, finely chopped

Peel the bananas, cut in half lengthways and dip in the lemon juice. Place the halved bananas in a flameproof casserole dish greased with half the butter, sprinkle with the sugar and pour over the rum. Cook over the heat for a few minutes. Add the cream, top with the chopped almonds and a few knobs of butter. Bake in the oven at 220°C/425°F/gas mark 7 for 15 minutes.

PEARS WITH CREAM

Serves 4

4 pears, peeled, cored and cubed
100 g/4 oz icing sugar
50 g/2 oz butter
150 ml/¹/4 pint cream
25 g/1 oz almonds, chopped and toasted

Place the cubed pears in a greased ovenproof dish. Top with the sugar and the

Top: Pears with Raisins
Bottom: Bananas with Cream

butter cut into small pieces. Bake in the oven at 220°C/425°F/gas mark 7 for 15 minutes until the pears begin to turn golden. Cover with the cream and return to the oven for a further 3 minutes. Top with the chopped almonds and serve.

CHESTNUT SOUFFLÉ

Serves 4

¹/2 kg/1 lb chestnuts
¹/2 litre/³/4 pint milk
1 vanilla pod
150 g/5 oz sugar
3 eggs, separated

To peel the chestnuts, score a cross on the side of each nut. Boil for a few minutes then drain, and while still warm peel off the hard outer shell and furry inner skin. Simmer the chestnuts in the milk with the vanilla pod for 20 minutes. Stir in the sugar until dissolved. Remove the vanilla pod and rub the mixture through a sieve to make a purée. Add the egg yolks. Beat the egg whites until stiff and fold in. Pour the mixture into a greased soufflé dish and bake in the oven at 190°C/375°F/gas mark 5 for 30 minutes.

DRIED FRUIT AND NUT BAKE

Serves 4

4 eggs, separated
100 g/4 oz sugar
100 g/4 oz flour
grated rind of 1 lemon
50 g/2 oz currants, soaked in hot water
25 g/1 oz almonds, chopped
25 g/1 oz walnuts, chopped
25 g/1 oz hazelnuts, chopped

Beat the egg yolks with half the sugar. Add the flour and grated lemon rind. Beat the egg whites until stiff and fold in with the remaining sugar. Mix together well then add the drained soaked currants and the nuts. Pour the mixture into a greased mould and bake in the oven at 180°C/350°F/gas mark 4 for 45 minutes.

STUFFED APPLES

Serves 4

¹/4 kg/¹/2 lb short-grain rice
25 g/1 oz sugar
60 g/2¹/2 oz butter
¹/2 litre/³/4 pint milk

4 apples
1 tsp cinnamon
4 dessertspoons honey
4 dessertspoons chopped walnuts
10 dessertspoons currants, soaked in hot water

Place the rice, sugar and a knob of the butter in a saucepan with the milk. Simmer for 30 minutes until the rice is cooked. Meanwhile, cut the tops off the apples, and scoop out the flesh using a teaspoon. Sauté the apple flesh and cinnamon in the remaining butter until soft. When the rice is cooked, add the honey, chopped walnuts, currants and cooked apple flesh. Fill the apple shells with this mixture and bake in the oven at 180°C/350°F/gas mark 4 for about 15 minutes. Serve warm or cold.

WALNUT SAUCE

Serves 4

¹/4 litre/7 fl oz milk
400 g/14 oz walnuts, chopped
2 slices toast, chopped
150 g/6 oz sugar

Place all the ingredients in a saucepan and simmer together for 45 minutes. Remove from the heat and allow to cool.

HAZELNUT PIE

Serves 4

1/4 kg/1/2 lb ground hazelnuts
100 g/4 oz butter
1/4 kg/1/2 lb sugar
grated rind of 1 lemon
pinch of cinnamon

Beat together all the ingredients until smooth and creamy. Lightly butter a shallow baking dish and turn the mixture into it. Bake in the oven at 180°C/350°F/gas mark 4 for about 25 minutes until golden.

PRESERVED FRUIT AND CURD CHEESE CAKE

Serves 6

1/2 kg/1 lb curd cheese
50 g/2 oz cornflour
grated rind of 1 lemon
6 dessertspoons sugar
125 g/4 oz butter, melted
100 ml/4 fl oz natural yoghurt
6 eggs, beaten
50 g/2 oz currants, soaked in hot water
200 g/7 oz whole preserved fruit, drained and chopped

In a mixing bowl, blend together the curd cheese, cornflour, rind, sugar and melted butter. Add the yoghurt, beaten eggs, drained soaked currants and chopped fruit. Pour the mixture into a cake tin greased with butter and bake in the oven at 180°C/350°F/gas mark 4 for 30 minutes until set.

LEMON CREAM

Serves 6

6 gelatine leaves
6 eggs, separated
juice of 3 lemons
100 g/4 oz sugar
150 ml/1/4 pint double or whipping cream, lightly whipped

Soak the gelatine in a little cold water. Meanwhile, beat the egg yolks with the sugar until a frothy cream is obtained. Add the lemon juice to the gelatine and heat until dissolved. Pour into the lemon mixture and chill until half set. Beat the egg whites until standing in soft peaks then fold into the lemon mixture with the lightly whipped cream. Pour into individual dishes and chill in the refrigerator until serving.

DANISH PLUMS

Serves 6

1 kg/2.2 lb plums
75 g/3 oz sugar
6 slices white bread, cubed
80 g/3 1/2 oz butter
150 ml/1/4 pint single or double cream
1 tsp cinnamon

Place the plums and sugar in a saucepan with just enough water to cover. Simmer gently until the plums are tender and the liquid is syrupy. Set aside to cool. Heat the butter in a frying pan and fry the bread over a low heat, stirring constantly, until lightly browned. Leave to cool. Just before serving, mix the cooked plums with the pieces of fried bread and pour into a bowl. Serve with cream and extra sugar for sprinkling.

ICE-CREAM SUNDAE

Serves 6

1/2 litre/3/4 pint vanilla ice-cream
250 g/8 oz redcurrants
250 g/8 oz raspberries
100 g/4 oz sugar
6 wafers

Remove the redcurrants from their stalks and hull the raspberries, if necessary. Layer the fruit and sugar in a bowl and chill for 2 hours. To serve, remove the ice-cream from the freezer and cut into 16 even-sized pieces. Fill 6 sundae glasses with the ice-cream, alternating with layers of fruit. Serve immediately.

APPLES WITH CINNAMON

Serves 4

1 1/2 kg/3 lb apples
200 g/7 oz sugar
100 ml/4 fl oz sweet sherry
grated rind and juice of 1 lemon
1 vanilla pod
1 cinnamon stick
icing sugar

Wash the apples, but do not peel them. Remove the stalks and the cores. Place the apples in a saucepan with just enough water to cover and the sugar, sherry, lemon rind and juice, vanilla pod and cinnamon stick. Cook over a low heat until the apples begin to go soft. Remove the apples from the pan and place on a serving dish. Boil the cooking liquid over a high heat until reduced and syrupy, then strain over the apples. Top with sifted icing sugar, if desired.

FIG DELIGHT

Serves 4

12 ripe figs
2 dessertspoons honey
100 ml/4 fl oz double or whipping cream, whipped lightly
50 g/2 oz almonds, finely chopped
50 g/2 oz walnuts, finely chopped

Carefully peel the figs and chop the flesh. Mix with the honey and cream and pour into individual serving dishes. Top each dish with the chopped almonds and walnuts and chill for at least 1 hour before serving.

Top: Apples with Cinnamon
Bottom: Fig Delight

INDEX